Pray

the Trail

A Contemplative Walk
on the Ocmulgee Heritage Trail

The Brainstorm Lab.com

Pray the Trail
A Contemplative Walk on the Ocmulgee Heritage Trail

Jim Dant
Photography, Mark Strozier

ISBN: 978-0-9821640-0-6

Printed in the United States of America

For

Lewis Jamiroquai Bigguhns

preface

Each year, over 75,000 pairs of feet find their way along the nine miles of pathway that cuts through the fourteen hundred acres of the Ocmulgee Heritage Trail. As the only riverside trail and park system in Middle Georgia, it provides a perfect setting for walking, running, bird-watching, biking and enjoying many of Macon's historic treasures like: Rose Hill Cemetery and the Ocmulgee Heritage Monument.

While an obvious setting for recreation, author Jim Dant and photographer Mark Strozier have also found the trail to be a natural sanctuary for contemplation and prayer. This small book moves the reader – meditation by meditation – along the trail. Beginning at Gateway Park and journeying north to Jackson Springs Park, the reader is given opportunity, at recognizable sites, to stop, rest and reflect upon many of life's significant blessings and challenges.

Carry the book while walking the trail or simply enjoy the trail through the artful eye of photographer Mark Strozier. Allow the sites and Psalms and prayers to speak to you. Be blessed...

Alpha and Omega,
God of all beginnings and all ends,
My feet are not the first to tread
this trail beside the river.
Rising high, just to the south, are mounds
of memories.

Life has been lived
along these banks in moccasins
and Birkenstocks and wing-tipped
leather loafers.
Death has garnered grief.
Dreams have been dreamed,
found, forgotten.

Bless those who have walked before me.
Bless those who walk with me.
Bless those who will follow me.
Bless me as I walk this day.
Amen.

Imagine those who have walked beside this river be-fore you. Look around at those who've happened here today. Imagine those who will be here tomorrow. Pray God's blessings into their lives...and yours.

God of all creation
(and creativity),
Your Holy Muse has come to every generation.
David's harp and lyric flair
poured forth the psalms that soothe the soul.

With playful point and counterpoint,
Bach fashioned fugues
that feed us still.

And from this skyline
rhythms rise -
Reddings and Richard and Allmans
and others.

Tunes that start us tapping
and smiling and singing and laughing and hoping
your Holy Muse keeps meeting us here.
Meet us here.
Amen

Hum to yourself…or sing out loud…your favorite
song. Be thankful for the joyful, healing gift of music.

O God of Sabbath rest,
I hardly feel like sitting down;
slowing my pace in so young a journey.
But I'm not in a race.
Every moment must be savored.
Let me flow - slow - like the Ocmulgee.
Slow me down, Lord.
Slow me down.
Slow me.
Slow.
Amen.

prayer

meditation

Sit down. Relax. Rest. Take time to listen…even if this is your last stop today.

Transcendent God,
The wind blows through these branches.
Thick thoughts flow through my brain.
I think I hear your voice.
Or is it mine?
My thoughts are not your thoughts
and my ways are not your ways.
It's hard to know.
I revere the mystery of your distance.
I've waited, watched and wanted.
But like Elijah's chair,
The other bench has been too empty
far too long.
Meet me here…please.
Amen.

Dark nights – and dark days – of the soul are diffi-
cult to manage. Sit. Question. Lament. Wait. Listen.
Trust..

O Source of Freedom,
The high road and the low road
provide
different ventures - different views.
I've been told both roads reconcile
further up. Further up
beyond the line of my finite sight.

I've chosen.
They've chosen.

May I not judge
those who choose the other.
(Secretly I've envied.)
May others not judge me.
Amen.

What person or group of people have you judged, condemned or even hated? Pray for them…and perhaps… determine to meet, understand and even love them.

Loving Shepherd,
Stone stacked to my left
Underneath a breeze-blown banner and
metal moving to my right are
stark and raucous reminders
I am not alone in this world.
Offices and autos, all over the globe,
are filled with neighbors, friends and strangers
(and other folk under other flags).
Moving, rolling, working, surviving.
Needy souls
who, in some strange way,
are all a part of my world – my life,
your pasture.
Amen.

Pray for the individuals and families who are passing
in their cars. Pray for the employers, employees and
clients who inhabit the Macon skyline.

"...he blesses your children..."

Psalm 147:13b

God of all generations,
Before me,
a playground filled with children
in the shade of a forest
bent by wind and water and age.
The guardians of life
hovering over toe-headed boys
and the braided, beaded locks
of little girls.
Providing, protecting
in silent wisdom.
Amen.

prayer

meditation

Pray for the children you see. May they know heaven's protection and find life's purpose. Pray for their parents and grandparents and great grandparents and other caregivers who guard and guide and love them.

"In you, O Lord, do I put my trust..."

Psalm 31:1a

O God, my rock,
Columns hold the traffic
of a thousand days
and nights.
Planted deep
in mud and
clay and sand, they stand.

The columns of my life
are just as sure,
(and just as hidden
from the traveling masses.)
Help me to trust what I rarely,
if ever, see.
Amen.

prayer

Traffic travels over these columns everyday. Rarely do
drivers question the strength of the street. They simply drive...trusting. Trust God. Trust life.

"...your rod and your staff – they comfort me."

Psalm 23:4b

O Guardian of my soul,
Rails along the river walk
guard me, guide me,
hold me in.
Like lyricists (of old)
I'm prone to wander,
Lord, I feel it.
And while wandering is
yearning, learning and celebrating
the breadth of life,
(I need freedom)
I also need boundaries.
Hold me in.
Amen.

prayer

meditation

When has your adventurous spirit brought joy to your life? When have overly restrictive boundaries robbed you of life's joy? In what areas of life to do you need more boundaries? Determine to live your life with a healthy, joyful balance.

"...you cover all their sin."

Psalm 85:2b

Spirit of God,
The kudzu covers
post and pole
and transforms
common things
into leafy living sculptures -
invasive, all consuming, life.
But deep down, beneath green life,
post and pole remain.

Holy Spirit
cover me. Invade my
soul and skin and mind
with your invasive, all consuming life.
And in the process let me be –
help me become
me.
Amen.

prayer

meditation

We are earthy and spiritual. We are a cosmic mix of
dirt and spirit. We can rid ourselves of neither. The
best we can hope for – the best we can achieve – is a
beautiful blending of the two.

"How lovely is your dwelling place, O Lord of hosts!"

Psalm 84:1

O God of nature,
Exposed bough-beams arch overhead
(a cathedral carved from bark and limb)
allowing skylight to come in
and light the concrete carpet
on which I tread.

No narthex ever looked so grand
(with marble tile and chiseled rail)
as this cathedral of the trail
where light and presence touch
the place I stand.
Amen.

Thank God for the holy places of your life.

"How good and pleasant it is when kindred live together in unity!"

Psalm 133:1

Prince of Peace,
Rows of granite rise
from blades of grass. Fescue
fertilized by blades of another kind.
Steel that severed flesh from bone,
and brother from brother, and friend
from friend.

Now, we are fighting over what
we fought over.
And the rows of granite rise
from blades of grass. Rescue
us, O Lord.
Amen.

With whom are you presently in conflict? Pray for them. Forgive them. Release your anger. Be free… and live.

"If I ascend to heaven, you are there; if I make my bed in hell, you are there."

Psalm 139:8

O God, of the living and the dead,
I stand on the banks of the river
and stare
at the steps and terraces
that rise and fall before me
just on the other side.
They form a path amid the graves
that rise toward blue sky.
You are there.
You are there with those
who've crossed the river,
climbed the stairway to heaven, and
have found eternal rest,
just on the other side.
Amen

"Yea, though I walk through the valley…"

Psalm 23:4a

O God of heaven and earth,
I'm tired of ups and downs.
(Especially downs.)

Every once in a while,
It's nice to see a bridge
That moves from height to height
And avoids the valley.

I thank you for those ditches
I have avoided. Some by luck.
Some by providence.
Others by the careful work
of those who bridge my path.
Amen.

prayer

meditation

We have struggled, but we have not experienced every struggle. Luck, providence and the good work of others has helped us avoid many valleys. What's the best day you can remember? Give thanks for the good days.

"Your word is a lamp unto my feet and a light unto my path."

Psalm 119:105

O Living Word,
You light my path
from dusk to dawn –
dark moments, heavy loads
lightened with a word.
From sacred page
(and ancient sage or even the voice
of a friend)
comes radiant sounds
that scatters fear
(and other unseen night-time pests.)
Amen.

prayer

Reflect upon the wisest words that you have heard. Let your mind wander to sacred texts, the repetitive words of parents and grandparents, and the encouraging words of friends. Be thankful for words that illumine.

"I will render thank offerings to you, for you have delivered my soul from death..."

Psalm 56:12b-13a

Beautiful Savior,
What lies beneath another's soul
where days and years of soil
cover secrets – packed
and pressed
and trampled on?

What courage calls forth
images
to rise from crusty,
heart-shaped graves
and show themselves –
bejeweled stones?

How might I carve
or color stone
to shout or whisper to
the world the depth of pain
and height of my deliverence?
Amen.

In your mind's eye, envision your favorite piece of art. What does it tell you of the artist's personal pain or joy? Thank God for those who have the courage to sculpt and sketch the secrets of their soul.

"Your ancestors tested me, and forced me to prove myself, even though they had seen my work. For forty years, I loathed that genera-tion..."   Psalm 95:9-10b

Eternal God,
Do we bring drama to your life?
Gazing up,
the elm branches bring
contour and contrast
decorating a monochromatic heaven.

What would your life be
without us? Without our
messes and moans and wide-eyed wonder
(and embarrassingly humorous humanity),
Do we bring drama to your life,
Eternal God?
Amen.

At our best – and perhaps at our worst – we color heaven. We give God something to do. When do you think heaven has laughed at you? Chided you? Helped You?

"Those who trust in the Lord are like Mount Zion, which cannot be moved, but abides forever."

Psalm 125:1

O Root of Jesse,
You are planted deep
in the history of all time
and Mount Zion rises high above
the pathways of holy land –
immovable.
My life moves.

Flat boats once moved north and south
and then a train and now a plane
flys overhead reminding me that
change defines the essence of my time.
My life moves.
Give me roots
or move with me
Root of Jesse.
Amen.

prayer

meditation

What changes have you recently endured in your life? Where is your life rooted? How have these roots helped you deal with change?

O God, my friend,
I see a name I recognize
in herringbone beneath my feet.
Awkward letters let me know
these characters were carved long ago
when my dear friend was just a child.

I've seen her now in cap and gown
and she has gone, to make her mark,
on people and places other than brick
that lies in herringbone beneath my feet.

I hope that she remembers me
(as I remember her) and some word
or smile or gesture made
made a difference in her life
the way that others made a difference in me
when I was making awkward letters.
Amen.

prayer

Thank God for those who have influenced your life.
Thank God for those whom you have the opportunity
to influence. Live well.

Mighty God,
In times past,
you've raised your hand
high and hard against us
plaguing us with locust, lice,
and bloody water flowing through
another river.

Tears and terror filled a night
when firstborn children silent laid
in loving arms of those who lived
beneath the power of oppression,
above the suffering of the slaves –
middle class.

Passover.
Hundreds of cars pass over this trail.
Passengers plagued by perennial pain
fostered by fault (or no reason at all
except they live in this world's domain.)
Be gracious to us, Mighty God,
we who live this side of the sea.
May pain pass over those
on the overpass.
Amen

Pray that God will bring some solace to the hearts of
those who pass over you…on the overpass.

"Turn my eyes from looking at vanities; give me life in your ways."

Psalm 119:37

Redeeming God,
Retreating is not giving up,
but rather resting for return.
My travels on this trail have been in vain
if in some way, large or small,
I have not been transformed.

The path ends paces up ahead
where concrete meets pavement
and park meets homes.
I must soon return to these streets,
plunging back into the mass
of people and priorities
that grace the canvas of my life.

I have retreated.
Help me return
with renewed vision
within and without.
Amen

Gaze at the street before you – a home, a car, a stranger. How has your vision changed during your time on the trail?

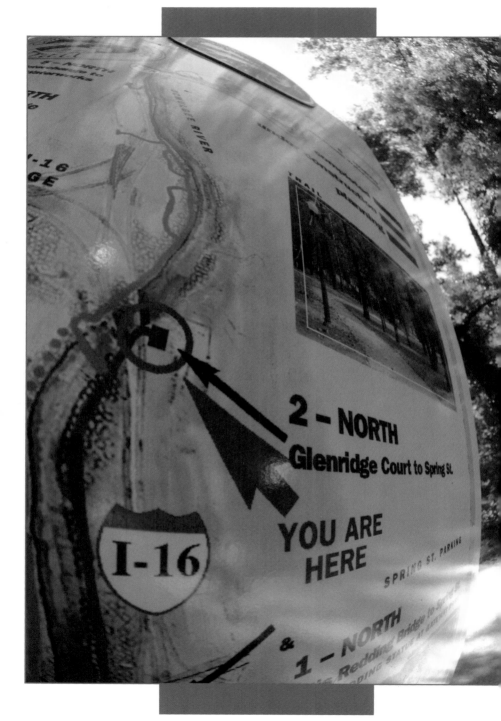

psalm

"O that I had wings like a dove! I would fly away and be at rest."

Psalm 55:6

Guiding Spirit,
I am here.
I am here in my marriage,
in my career, in my friendships,
in my finances, in my thoughts,
in my growth, in my travel
on the trail.

I am here.
Footprints lie behind me
marking moments of fun
and failure, ecstasy and ache,
passion and pain.
Where do I go from here?
Guide me Great Jehovah.
Amen

prayer

meditation

Where are you now? Where do you want to be? Go there. Go with God.